Michael & Peter Bento

MW01016814

Picture
Poems

Rocky View School Division
Media Services
Professional Collection

Hodder & Stoughton

A MEMBER OF THE HODDER HEADLINE GROUP

ACKNOWLEDGEMENTS

Poems

Most of the poems were specially commissioned by the publisher. Copyright remains with the individual poets. The poets may be contacted through The Poetry Society, 22 Betterton Street, London WC2H 9BU.

The publisher would like to thank the following poets and publishers for permission to reproduce copyright material: 'Breughel in Naples' is reprinted by permission of The Peters Fraser and Dunlop Group Limited on behalf of © Dannie Abse. The poem was first published in *Remembrance of Crimes Past*, 1990 Hutchinson. 'The Avenue after Hobbema' © Vicki Feaver appeared in *The Handless Maiden*, Jonathan Cape, 1994.'Child with a Dove' © George Harrison, first published in *Posting Letters*, OUP, 1968. 'A Poem is a Painting' © Phoebe Hesketh, first published in *The Leave Train: New and Selected Poems*, Enitharmon Press, 1994. 'Painter and Poet' and 'Woman Ironing' © U.A. Fanthorpe, appeared in *Safe as Houses*(1995), reproduced by permission of Peterloo Poets.'Vase/Faces - A Pantoum' © Colin Rowbotham appeared in *Touchstones 4*, Hodder & Stoughton and in *Strange Estates*, The Rockingham Press, 1994.
p. 72 Many thanks to Sally Butcher for recording the dialogue between Sophie and Simon.

Paintings/pictures

Tate Gallery p.8 British School, 17th Century: The Cholmondely Sisters; Sonia Boyce p.10 Sonia Boyce: Big Woman's Talk; Musees Royaux des Beaux-Arts de Beligique, Brussels/Bridgeman Art Library, London p.12 Pieter Brueghel: Landscape with the Fall of Icarus; Tate Gallery Publications p.16 Salvador Dali: Metamorphosis of Narcissus; Musee d'Orsay, Paris/Giraudon/Bridgeman Art Library, London p.18 Edgar Degas: Fin d'Arabesque; National Gallery, London/Bridgeman Art Library, London p.20 Edgar Degas: Lala at the Fernando Circus; Walker Art Gallery, Liverpool/Bridgeman Art Library, London p.22 Edgar Degas: La Repasseuse (Woman Ironing); Cordon Art p.24 M.C. Escher: Drawing Hands; Courtesy Jay Jopling London p.26 and 70 © Antony Gormley: European Field; National Gallery, London/Bridgeman Art Library, London p.28 Meindert Hobbema: The Avenue at Middelharnis; National Gallery, London/Bridgeman Art Library, London p.30 William Hogarth: The Graham Children; Sheffield City Art Galleries/Bridgeman Art Library, London p.32 Gwen John: A Corner of the Artist's room, Paris; Tate Gallery Publications p.34 Wassily Kandinsky: Swinging; Art Institute of Chicago/Bridgeman Art Library, London p.36 Rene Magritte: Time Transfixed; Lauros-Giraudon/Bridgeman Art Library, London p.39 Rene Magritte: Golconda; Bildarchiv Preusssischer Kulturbesitz, Berlin p.40 Claude Monet: Spring Landscape; National Gallery, London/Bridgeman Art Library, London p.41 Pablo Picasso: Child With Dove; Museum of Modern Art p.42 Pablo Picasso: The Three Musicians; Wallace Collection, London/Bridgeman Art Library, London p.44 Hermensz van Rijn Rembrandt: Portrait of Titus; Manchester City Art Galleries p.46 Stanley Spencer: A Village in Heaven; Walker Art Gallery p.48 Marianne Stokes: Polishing Pans; Kettle's Yard, University of Cambridge p.49 Alfred Wallis: Penzance Harbour; Ashmolean Museum, Oxford p.50 Paolo Uccello: A Hunt in a Forest; Tate Gallery, London p.52 James Abbott McNeill Whistler: Miss Cicely Alexander: Harmony in Grey and Green; Wallace Collection, London/Bridgeman Art Library, London p.54 Diego Rodriguex de Silva y Velazquez: Prince Baltasar Carlos in Silver; National Gallery, London p.56 Joseph Wright of Derby: An Experiment on a Bird in the Air-pump; Christie's Images p.58 Giacometti: L'homme Qui Marche (Walking Man); Kunsthistorisches Museum/Bridgeman Art Library, London p.59 Giuseppe Arcimboldo: Water; Christie's Images/Bridgeman Art Library, London p.60 Katsushika Hokusai: The Great Wave of Kanagawa; Museum of Modern Art p.61 Andrew Wyeth: Christina's World; Giraudon/Bridgeman Art Library, London p.62 Henri Matisse: Flight of Icarus; Tate Gallery p.63 F.N. Souza: Crucifixion; Tate Gallery p.64 Jasper Johns: 0-9.

British Library Cataloguing in Publication Data

Benton, Michael, 1939–
   Picture poems
   1. Children's poetry, English   2. Art and literature –
   Juvenile literature
   I. Title   II. Benton, Peter, 1942–
   821.9'14

ISBN 0 340 679875

First published 1997
Impression number   10 9 8 7 6 5 4
Year   2006 2005 2004

Copyright © 1997 Michael and Peter Benton

All rights reserved. No part of this publication may be reproduced or transmitted in any form or by any means, electronic or mechanical, including photocopy, recording, or any information storage and retrieval system, without permission in writing from the publisher or under licence from the Copyright Licensing Agency Limited. Further details of such licences (for reprographic reproduction) may be obtained from the Copyright Licensing Agency Limited, of 90 Tottenham Court Road, London W1T 4LP.

Typeset by Wearset, Boldon, Tyne and Wear
Printed in Dubai for Hodder & Stoughton Educational, a division of Hodder Headline ,
338 Euston Road, London NW1 3BH.

Contents

CONTENTS

Gallery

Making Connections

Gallery Information

Introduction

Picture Poems is a collection of poems, inspired mainly by paintings but also by drawings and sculptures. The aim of the book and its predecessors for older pupils, *Double Vision* and *Painting with Words*, is to encourage cross-curricular work by studying paintings and sculptures and the poems which have been inspired by them. It is suitable for work with pupils at Key Stages 2 and 3 in English, Art and related national curriculum subjects.

Most of the poems in this collection have been specially commissioned, many of the poets taking up our invitation to write about the pictures we suggested, others making their own choices the subjects of new poems, some doing both. We are delighted to be able to bring so much exciting new material to the classroom. A further bonus has been that some of the poets chose the same work of art to respond to and as a result we can print two or more poems about the same painting. This enables the pupil to experience different responses to a single image.

The practice of writing poems about works of art has a long history; Keats's *Ode on a Grecian Urn* and Browning's *My Last Duchess* are famous examples from the last century. Both poems are about imaginary works. Every poem in this book is about an actual painting or sculpture which pupils can study in its reproduced form here or, as circumstances allow, view in an art gallery.

The material is arranged in three sections:

- The **Anthology** displays 27 pictures with the poems that have been inspired by them.
- The **Gallery** features a number of pictures for pupils to write their own poems about.
- **Making Connections** has two parts:

    I Teaching Ideas which looks at eight pictures from the **Anthology** section in detail and makes suggestions for lessons and homework;

    II Themes and Projects which is a brief outline of general themes and projects suitable for more extended work.

The **Anthology** is arranged alphabetically by artist wherever possible. We could have arranged the material thematically, or chronologically by painter or poet, or by some supposed degree of difficulty but the advantage of the way we have chosen is the juxtaposing of all the poems relating to a particular painting. It also places more emphasis on the teacher's judgement about which pairings are most suitable for their classes. We hope, too, that the arbitrary alphabetical order allows the singular appeal of these painting/poem combinations to speak for themselves. For this reason we have also kept the **Anthology** section free from teaching approaches, preferring to collect these together in **Making Connections.***

The **Anthology** shows poets adopting many different stances and voices as they write about the pictures:

- Narratives are told as third-person accounts as in Heather Harvey's *Narcissus – a sonnet*;
- as first-person reflections of the poet as in Gillian Clarke's *European Field*;
- as the day-dreams of the painter in Michael Benton's *Alfred Wallis Day-Dreams in the Bath*;
- as the thought-track of the sitter in Sylvia Kantaris's *Growing Pains*;
- as the interior monologue of the viewer in Gregory Harrison's *Child with a Dove*;
- as dialogues between depicted figures in different paintings as in Anna Adams's *Prince Baltasar Carlos in Silver and Miss Cicely Alexander*; or between painter and sitter as in U.A. Fanthorpe's *Woman Ironing*; and as one half of a desperate dialogue on a mobile phone in Gareth Owen's *Icarus by Mobile*.

Some poems literally speak out for the paintings, including conversation or comment in their lines; others maintain a mood of quiet contemplation. Some operate in the fictive time of the depicted scene; others in the real time of the viewer interpreting the artist's work. Some take in the whole atmosphere or subject of the painting; others concentrate on one or two significant details. By talking and writing about these poems and pictures and by comparing their own responses with those of the poets, pupils can develop insights into how these two art forms create their effects. A natural corollary to such study is for pupils to write their own poems about pictures; in order to encourage this, we have included a small **Gallery** of paintings towards the end of the book.

Finally, each section of the book is introduced by a poem which itself is a commentary upon what follows. Phoebe Hesketh's *A Poem is a Painting* at the start of the book, opens with an epigraph from Leonardo da Vinci and closes with the idea that poems come alive with the imaginative participation of the reader in the 'spaces between the words'. The **Gallery** is introduced by R.S. Thomas's poem of that name, one which reverses the roles of the viewer and the viewed and questions the values we attach to art. **Making Connections** is prefaced by a humorous poem by U.A. Fanthorpe: we hope our overall presentation in the book avoids the feeling of the 'set text' that this poem pokes fun at, and that the teaching ideas encourage pupils to 'invest in the poet' as well as in the painter.

Michael and Peter Benton

* Where this symbol ⌒ appears alongside the picture title, it indicates that further information and teaching suggestions can be found in **Making Connections** (pp 65–76).

ANTHOLOGY

— A Poem is a Painting —

A poem is a painting that is not seen;
A painting is a poem that is not heard.

That's what poetry is –
a painting in the mind.
Without palette and brush
it mixes words into images.
The mind's edge sharpens the knife
slashing the canvas with savage rocks
twisting trees and limbs into tortuous shapes
as Van Gogh did
or bewitched by movement's grace,
captures the opalescent skirts
of Degas' ballet dancers.

But words on the page
as paint on canvas
are fixed.
It's in the spaces between
the poem is quickened.

Phoebe Hesketh

BRITISH SCHOOL, *The Cholmondeley Sisters*, 1600–1610, The Tate Gallery (London), oil on panel, 88.9 × 172.5 cm

— The Twins —

Who are these Ladies, painted there
With sharp black eyes and trim black hair,
And in their arms across their laps,
Two babies dressed in long red wraps?

Four hundred years ago there were
Two Ladies born near Lancashire;
We don't know either Lady's name,
We only know they looked the same,
In fact, alike as two smart pins.
– So no one doubts that they were twins.
And later on, or so it's said,
On the same day the two were wed,
And even odder, not long after,
One had a son and one a daughter
– And these two babies, bright and new,
Were born upon the same day too.
No one had planned all these events,
They happened by coincidence,
But seeing it turned out that way,
Their Lords decided, one fine day,
To have a double portrait done.
One took her daughter, one her son,
And all that day and all that week
They sat there, not allowed to speak
– The babies neither slept nor cried –
Until their Lords were satisfied
To see their ladies, finished there,
Propped up on pillows grey and square,
Their babies pointing to their right,
With open eyes – as black and bright
As either's mother's had, or aunt,
All of them looking elegant,
And proud to let the artist make
This picture for the future's sake,
Just so that all the world could see
A portrait of this family.

– I hope they thanked him. Properly.

Alan Brownjohn

SONIA BOYCE, *Big Woman's Talk*, 1984, Private Collection, pastel and ink on paper, 148 × 155 cm

— Big Woman's Talk —

(with thanks to Sonia Boyce)

Children should be seen and not heard
Grandma says,
Be invisible
I say.
Secret as silence in a submarine
Take soundings.

I told her look before you leap!
  There are none so deaf as those who will not hear.
When children are little they make our heads ache,
when grown, our hearts.
  But it's no use crying over spilt milk.
Still waters run deep.

And little pitchers have big ears.

Beverley Naidoo

— Justice —

Justice
Just is
That.
Just Ice.
If I could find words enough
To express
My pain
Or worth enough
To heal the humiliation
Or breath enough
To sigh and let it all
                    slip
                        away –
That would be justice.
But Justice
Just is not like
That.
Suffer while the wounds heal
Despair while the tears dry
And show yourself
as they see you
      Just ice
        That
            is your
                Justice.

Olusola Oyeleye

PIETER BRUEGHEL, *Landscape with the Fall of Icarus*, c.1555–58, Musées Royaux des Beaux-Arts de Belgique (Brussels), oil on canvas, 73.5 × 112 cm

— *Icarus by Mobile* —

Daddy, Daddy is that you?
Listen I don't have much time OK.
But I wanted to say, right
It's back to the drawing board Daddy
The whole contraption is a no no.
The wings?
No, the wings worked fine
Couldn't fault the wings in any way
The wings were ace
And your calculations on the stresses
Re wind and feathers
Spot on!

Likewise the pinion tolerances
And remember that flap factor
That gave us both such sleepless nights
Let me tell you
Those flaps worked like a dream.
But Daddy
Oh Daddy
How could you forget the sun!
I don't have much time
So listen OK.
We're talking equations here
Just let me spell it out for you:
Solar heat + bees wax + ambition =
Total Meltdown and I mean total
Which equals, to put it simply,
Your boy Icarus on collision course
With something called the Earth.
Daddy I don't have much time
Let me give you my co-ordinates
For the pick up
OK stretch of headland and a bay
Visibility good, outlook calm
And hey
Am I lucky
Or am I lucky!
There's a galleon anchored near the shore
Looks like Icarus
Is in for an early pick up this fine morning.
And over there some poor old farmer's
Ploughing through a field of stones
And here's an old boy with a fishing pole and
Listen Daddy
Would you believe
Some guy just out of frame
Is painting the whole thing.
And now I'm waving Daddy, waving
Any minute now they'll all look up and
So listen Daddy I don't have much time
I'm going to start screaming soon OK.
Can you still hear me?
I don't have much
Daddy, I just wanted to ask
You know
About my mum
Was she
Listen Daddy
I don't have much time
I

Gareth Owen

PIETER BRUEGHEL, *Landscape with the Fall of Icarus* (details)

— *Brueghel in Naples* —

'About suffering they were never wrong,
The Old Masters . . . ' – W H Auden

Ovid would never have guessed how far
and Father's notion about wax melting, bah!
It's ice up there. Freezing.
Soaring and swooping over solitary altitudes
I was breezing along (a record I should think)
when my wings began to moult not melt.
These days, workmanship, I ask you.
Appalling.

There's a mountain down there on fire
and I'm falling, falling away from it.
Phew, the sun's on the horizon
or am I upside down?

Great Bacchus, the sea is rearing
up. Will I drown? My white legs
the last to disappear? (I have no trousers on.)
A little to the left the ploughman,
a little to the right a galleon,
a sailor climbing the rigging,
a fisherman casting his line,
and now I hear a shepherd's dog barking.
I'm that near.

Lest I leave no trace
but a few scattered feathers on the water
show me your face, sailor,
look up, fisherman,
look this way, shepherd,
turn around, ploughman.
Raise the alarm! Launch a boat!

My luck. I'm seen
only by a jackass of an artist
interested in composition, in the green
tinge of the sea, in the aesthetics
of disaster – not in me.

I drown, bubble by bubble,
(Help! Save me!)
while he stands ruthlessly
before the canvas, busy busy,
intent on becoming an Old Master.

Dannie Abse

SALVADOR DALI, *Metamorphosis of Narcissus,* 1937, The Tate Gallery (London), oil on canvas, 51.1 × 78.1 cm

— *Narcissus – a sonnet* —

He finds a quiet pool one stormy day
As clouds glare green and orange in the heat
He's all alone; his friends are far away,
His dog is tired. He stoops and cools his feet.

The water gleams, reflecting back a face
As lovely as a flower. No longer free,
He'll stay for ever in this magic place,
Crying for love's impossibility.

And so he bends and gazes, growing more pale,
Knowing his neck, his back, his arm, his leg,
(All changing over and over and hour by hour)
Will make a finger, knuckle, thumb and nail,
And be the careful hand that holds the egg
From which is born one pale and lovely flower.

Heather Harvey

— *Only Dali, or the Gods* —

(After *The Metamorphosis of Narcissus*)

Narcissus, golden and disgraced,
misshapen, sinks his arms and legs
into the luminous turquoise water,
remembers sadly how he embraced
his own reflection, caught the weeds
and shadows in his manly arms.

Now he's stuck forever
somewhere between
night and day,
death and life,
ugliness and beauty.
Even the rocks and pools
have nightmares here.

Only Dali, or the gods
could create a land
of such teasing strangeness
for one who loved himself too much.

A statue gazes on an empty chequer-board.
Blood-red sands will burn your fingers off.
A scaly, prehistoric dog gnaws on scarlet.
Through the wrong end of a telescope, a ring
of tiny, disappointed ghosts surrounds a lake.

On the dark bank Narcissus' true reflection
is a giant, cracked, ant-infested hand.
The chiselled thumb, taller than a man,
balances an egg, hatching into a flower.
Brave and pale and delicate,
a narcissus sprouts from his stone head.

Moniza Alvi

SALVADOR DALI, *Metamorphosis of Narcissus* (details)

EDGAR DEGAS, *Fin d'Arabesque,* 1877, Musée D'Orsay (Paris), pastel, 67 × 38 cm

— Fin d'Arabesque *by Edgar Degas* —

She is that special image of dance.
Other dancers are at ease off-stage.
She ends a programme and highlights it.

Clean, in the music's rhythms,
her lines of movements had all stood out
in performance with the company.

Now, concealing tiredness and aches
she performs end like beginning:
controlled, skilled, graceful.

Open armed, she holds out her bouquet
marking body discipline applauded
for the triumph of dance.

And arms, legs, costume, encircling her,
she looks dreamlike, as if she blooms
under leaves-filtered moonlight.

James Berry

— Fin d'Arabesque —

At last I whirl and balance on one toe –
The audience roars!
Not waiting 'til the music ends,
Their applause bursts into the air.
They jump out of their seats,
Raising towards me their smiling faces,
Their cheers, their clapping hands.

The other dancers drift away,
As I step forward modestly
And curtsey, spreading my arms.
My hair is long and black,
My shoulders bare and creamy-white,
I wear tiny pink shoes,
And a dress like cobwebs, gold and silver

People are throwing flowers,
And everyone loves me
Because I am beautiful,
And this time I have done everything right.

We have finished looking at that picture.
I move on with the rest of the class,
Tugging up my grey socks.

Heather Harvey

EDGAR DEGAS, Miss *LaLa at the Fernando Circus*, 1879, The National Gallery (London), oil on canvas, 117 × 77.5 cm

— *Look, no hands* —

THE ARTIST: It was hard doing this. I had to go up near the roof,
Among the girders and dusty bits. And I had to keep
On trying till I found the right place to be –
Left, and in front; not very far below her
So I could make you see how hard it is.

You have to imagine the audience. I didn't
Bother with them, they're always the same,
Ooh-ing, aah-ing, clapping, some of them
Shutting their eyes. And the smells. You have
To imagine them too: people, horses, sawdust, sweat.

You're lucky. I'm showing you what the audience
Can't really see. Far off, up in the roof,
Something between a bird and an angel, using
Arms like wings. Hovering, you could say;
Not holding on. See how she does it?

Neither a bird nor an angel, she flies
With a metal bar in her teeth. And that strong mouth
Hauls her up, up, up, in her white and gold,
So that it all looks easy. So that she flies.

THE ARTISTE: All right, I suppose. Doesn't look much like me,
But it's me all right, my act. He's better
Than the usual gawpers. *How much d'you weigh?* they say,
Or *Are your teeth your own?* He painted my boots O.K.
I told him they cost a bomb.

U.A. Fanthorpe

La Repasseuse (Woman Ironing)

EDGAR DEGAS, *La Repasseuse (Woman Ironing)*, c.1880, Walker Art Gallery (Liverpool), oil on canvas, 81 × 63.5 cm

— *Woman Ironing** —

I thought I knew what was coming when he said
He wanted to do my likeness at the ironing.
I live in the city, people tell you things. Me looking at him,
It would be, across the ironing board, my hair and my eyes
In a good light, and something a bit off the shoulder.

But it wasn't. He rushed around drawing curtains.
Made it hard to iron. O yes, I had to keep ironing.
He needed to see the strength, he said. Kept on
About my dynamic right shoulder, then left it out,
Though you can see where he ought to have put it.

Come on, what's-your-name, he kept saying,
Show us that muscle-power! That's what I'm after.
I might've been an engine, not a person.
No, I didn't take to him. I'm used to rudeness,
But he was making such a sketch of me.

If someone's paying you, it isn't easy
To speak your mind. Still, *Sir*, I said,
I really don't want to see my hair like that,
All scraped back, like a hot person's hair,
And anyone can tell that under my arms I'm sweating.

Hair? Sweat? That's how it is when you iron,
Says he. *You're not here to tell me what to do.*
I'll make you permanent, the way you look
When you're ironing. O yes, he says, *I'll show you*
The way you look when no one's watching.

U.A. Fanthorpe

* The original title of this painting is *La Repasseuse.* The Walker Art Gallery translates this as *Woman Ironing,* which suggests to me a casual activity, like woman smiling. I'd think it more accurate if the painting were known as *Ironing Woman. Degas's ironers are trained specialists.

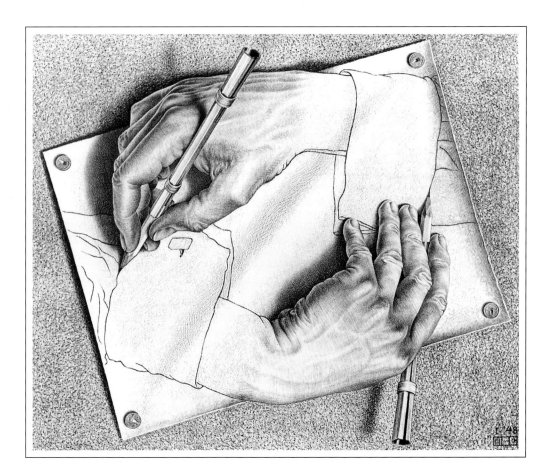

M.C. ESCHER,
Drawing Hands,
1948, Escher Foundation,
Haags Gemeentemuseum,
(The Hague),
lithograph, 28.5 × 34 cm

— *Drawing Hands – a Pantoum* —

Again your hand begins to draw
I feel my fingers live and warm
We sketch and shade the wrists, and more,
As each of each creates the form.

I feel my fingers live and warm
My life-blood flows in every vein
As each of each creates the form
We draw and pause, and draw again.

My life-blood flows in every vein
Be careful! you're creating ME!
We draw and pause, and draw again
We shape each other – both hands free!

Be careful! you're creating ME!
Don't make your lines too faint or rough
We shape each other – both hands free
But is this paper big enough?

Don't make your lines too faint or rough
We sketch and shade the wrists, and more,
But is this paper big enough?
Again your hand begins to draw.

Heather Harvey

ANON, *Vase/Faces*, 1915

— *Vase/Faces* —

To start with, you may realise
Two facing profiles, filled in black:
Like this. But is it otherwise?
They disappear and then are back:

Two facing profiles, filled in black,
Or should it be a jar of light?
They disappear and then are back.
The day is followed by the night.

Or should it be a jar of light?
It must be *this* or *that* you say.
The day is followed by the night,
But then the night precedes the day.

It must be *this* or *that* you say?
Why deal in terms like good and bad?
But then, the night precedes the day,
The two at once would drive you mad.

Why deal in terms like good and bad?
Why make a choice between the two?
The two at once would drive you mad,
That's all I have to say to you.

Why make a choice between the two?
Because we've done it all along;
That's all I have to say to you.
Of course, I could have got things wrong.

Because we've done it all along
Like this – but is it otherwise?
Of course, I could have got things wrong
To start with, you may realise.

Colin Rowbotham

— *European Field* —

– an installation by Antony Gormley

Thirty-five thousand faces in a field
the colour of clay and flesh and blood
crammed between clean white walls of a gallery.
Thirty-five thousand on tip-toe
craning their necks
breathing like a field of corn.

Thirty-five thousand voices asking
why, why, why
like wind in the grasses
of graveyards and old battlefields.
Seventy-thousand ears listening
to no answer.

We have paid to see them.
We did not expect to be stared at,
or that they would move in to live with us,
taking root in the field of our minds,
whispering all night
'we are you, you, you.'

Thirty-five thousand figures
crumbling in my head
to bones and dust and ashes
under a field of flowering grasses.

Galleries
should carry a health warning.

Gillian Clarke

ANTONY GORMLEY, *European Field* (details)

Aspects of Gormley's Field

(Tate Gallery, Liverpool)

Heads on bodies, heads with only eyes,
E.T. look-alikes minus feet or arms;
not one inch of space between
these sculpted clay figures
which give a warning voice
to our world, to ourselves
through eighty thousand eyes.
They stare up in appeal.   Disturb.

Arranged in rows, regimented
as though without choice,
they offer no sense of love
or mutual support, have become
lava from an eruption.
Eyes do not regard each other
only stare up in protest
at such diminution.   Sadden.

Did local people, who day by day
created these truncated bodies,
understand the power to be unleashed?
Sunbeams stress warmth of clay
deepen, lighten colours
as wind in a field of corn.
Here the many destroy the one
yet each speaks for the many.

Peggy Poole

[Left, and details above] ANTONY GORMLEY, *European Field*, 1995, The Tate Gallery (Liverpool), c. 35 000 clay figures, each 8–26 cm tall

MEINDERT HOBBEMA, *The Avenue at Middelharnis*, 1638–1709, The National Gallery (London), oil on canvas, 103.5 × 141 cm

— *The Avenue* —
after Hobbema

This land is so flat
the people who till these fields
still secretly refuse to believe
the world is round.

They plant cabbages and potatoes.
They keep a cow and a pig.
The men carve Meerschaum pipes.
Their women are embroiderers.

On summer evenings they walk out
between tall lines of poplars
brushing midges from their faces
with fat brown hands.

But every fifty years or so
someone tears himself away
from family and farm
and goes in search of the edge.   *Vicki Feaver*

Perspective is Bunk

The sky is high and blue,
    and shining in it is a daisy sun;
green ground lies down below,
    and in the space between

my house stands safe and square,
    and full of windows, curtains, and a door;
nice people live in there:
    Mummy, for sure.

She stands and smiles at me:
    she's most important, so she must be tall,
and when she walks away
    does not shrink small.

So my picture is true
    and better than this old one that pretends
it is an Avenue.
    I and my friends

know better. Leafy trees
    are tall and green, and people
are mostly person-size
    and nothing like a steeple.

Anna Adams

— The Mysteries of Perspective —

A 'V' of fuzzy clouds descends
as though two burning planes were falling
smokily, to crash where this land ends:
but these dark clouds are nothing so appalling.

If they are treetops, why are some so high,
and others dwindled small where tiny people
stand chatting under them? Fields meet the sky!
How comes it this man's taller than that steeple?

The white clouds up above extend wide wings
to bless a land where nothing's out of joint,
although art fools our eyes, cajoling things
to shrink by magic to a distant point.

The drainage ditches by the rutted track,
the level plain, well ruled by human reason,
all slide towards, and vanish through, the crack
that keeps its distance always: the horizon.

Anna Adams

WILLIAM HOGARTH, *The Graham Children*, 1697–1764, The National Gallery (London), oil on canvas, 160.5 × 181 cm

— *Captive Flesh* —

How long did you stand, pretty children,
in your frills and furbelows
while the artist painted the sheen of richness

and the bird beat its breast
against the bars
of the gilded cage?

Did none of you spy
the cat, ears focused for the faint
cries of captive flesh,

eyes wide as owls,
a grin of greedy satisfaction
savouring the morsel close enclosed?

Oh lucky stripey monster, you might cry,
claws scarring the leather of a studded chair,
poised to pounce

or, without a please or farewell,
spring out of the frame
into the freedom of a dark
night raiding.

Valerie Bird

WILLIAM HOGARTH, *The Graham Children*
(details)

GWEN JOHN, *A Corner of the Artist's Room, Paris,* 1876–1939, Sheffield City Art Galleries, oil on canvas, 31.7 × 26.7 cm

The Artist's Room – a painting by Gwen John

Where is she? Where?
Her old blue cardi's on the chair.
The window where she brushed her hair.

Her cushion, her white parasol,
the table where the sunlight fell
onto a sloping bedroom wall.

She isn't there, but this is where
she placed primroses in a jar
and gazed out at the evening star.

She stroked her cat, (he's out of sight),
took up her pen, began to write
how trees were great forests in the night.

Her cat is purring as it sleeps.
With canvas, oil and paint she keeps
her room alive for me. She dips

her sable brush in Naples yellow,
black, vermilion mixed with mellow
sunlight through a little window.

Lace curtains, table, flowers, chair,
prove to me that she was there.

Gillian Clarke

A corner of the Artist's Room, Paris
– by Gwen John

A background wall with window sunlight
and with warm triangular shapes
and a carpet with darker shades
feature a central chair and table
to illuminate squares and lines of a place.

Left there too, and not disturbed,
a huddled up parasol and shawl
contribute their own shapes
against an arm of the chair.

No magazines. No books. No papers.
The artist sits here, to think,
to explore, to find
that particular way to go on
making a painting.

And under repeated bodyweight
the chair's legs lost their straightness.
Have stressed and splayed a little.
But, today, no sitting in the chair.

And the picture glows with light.
Tones of shades and parts harmonise
a workplace and useful everyday things
and give pleasure like singing voices
mixed and well tuned.

James Berry

WASSILY KANDINSKY, *Swinging*, 1925, The Tate Gallery (London), oil on canvas, 70.5 × 50.2 cm

— *Swinging* —

(after *Swinging*, by Kandinsky)

We are building our world together,
Kandinsky and I –

a city of moons and lines and girders,
pens and pencils and planks of air.

We stroll through our patterned squares,
listening to grand announcements.

Under our white half-sun,
under our black sun,

we are cramming things in
and cutting them up,

experimenting with lilac,
swinging through melting red.

We are partners, Kandinsky and I.
Sometimes I feel like an apprentice,

practically useless – then he'll say
That orange tubing you found.

The thoughts you had yesterday.
Give them to me.

Let's add them to the painting.

Moniza Alvi

— *A Round – with Colours* —

. . . . silkily
In the light of the trim white moon the orange snakes wriggle
    primly
Over the red and yellow fruits the trim white moon sits
    tenderly
Above the ebony river the red and yellow fruits hang
    tremblingly
Under the new glow of the cloud-covered sun the ebony river lies
    stealthily
Touching the curves of the antelope's horns, the cloud-covered sun peers
    fearfully
Turning from the silver-tipped thorns, the antelope's horns toss
    furiously
Piercing the black-scarfed forest the silver-tipped thorns stab
    suddenly
Catching sight of blue-cheeked Winter the black-scarfed forest shivers
    silently
The orange snakes wriggle, as blue-cheeked winter greets the melting Spring . . . .

Heather Harvey

RENE MAGRITTE, *Time Transfixed*, 1939, The Art Institute of Chicago, oil on canvas, 146.4 × 97.5 cm

— *Time Transfixed* —

Time will stand still
When the lift in the multi storey
Rockets through the roof
And takes its place
Motionless amongst a million stars.

Time will stand still
When the cold March wind
Is weary of whistling
And suddenly stops –
A solid chunk of air.

Time will stand still
When a train hits the buffers,
Bursts through (to the amazement of pigeons)
And stands, its smoke frozen,
In my empty fireplace.

Heather Harvey

— Time Transfixed *by René Magritte* —

In the Thinking Room
at Childhood Hall,
the brown clock ticks
with the sound of the kiss
that my Grandma makes
against my cheek
again and again
when we first meet
after a week
of all the hours
that the brown clock's tick
has kissed away
today, to-
morrow, yesterday

are all the same
to the plum steam-train
that I sometimes hear
in the Thinking Room
at Childhood Hall –
it has no passengers at all,
till I grow old enough
and tall
to climb aboard
the plum steam-train
and blow a kiss
as I chuff away to to-
morrow, yesterday, today.

Carol Ann Duffy

— *Leaving Present* —

(Magritte's *Time Transfixed*)

The retirement clock: he's done his time,
now's the time for the time of his life,
for all the time in the world.
He places the clock where it can see him.

Time has always come in blocks. Now
it floods the landscape of his days,
runs through his fingers.
His thoughts dissolve in it like Disprin.

Time keeping's as unnecessary as he is.
He'd like to jump on a train to anywhere
but this blank-faced body-guard
is watching, its clipped, dry voice

foretelling mean time,
injury time, time out of mind,
the moment when his time
is up, is up, is up.

Carole Satyamurti

RENE MAGRITTE, *Time Transfixed* (detail)

RENE MAGRITTE, *Golconda*, 1953, Private Collection, oil on canvas, 79 × 98 cm

— *Time, Gentle Men* —

For a while, Magritte supported himself and his wife Georgette by designing wallpaper . . . (Marina Vaizey)

It's raining civil servants, taxmen, school inspectors
Gently falling earthward in bowler hats, dark overcoats,
Clutching identical briefcases in black-gloved hands.
What do they bring, I wonder? Do they feel anything?

Only the benefits of an ordered mind,
Where everything falls into place; the report is filed,
The books are balanced. The figures are agreed –
It is, very simply, an open and shut case.

But, maybe what we see is not a visitation
Rather a final audit, a calling to account
Of little men drawn up like dew from homes and offices,
Believing they have lived according to the book.

Solemnly, in neat black diamonds they ascend
To meet the Chief Inspector and their promised end.
Imprinting their repeated pattern on the sky,
It is our minds the silent swarm would occupy.

Peter Benton

CLAUDE MONET, *Summer*, 1874, Berlin Museums, oil on canvas, 57 × 80.3 cm

— *Printemps* —

*For a painting by Monet. (Suggested
by Joan Murray Simpson.)*

I kneel in the grass,
and my white skirt settles around me
soft as dandelion fluff.
My open parasol
is a green cup brimming with shade.
Poplars, in the light wind,
are turning hand over hand –
green side to white, over and under.
Further up the field
my little sister watches and listens
to the hidden life below –
a sense of wonder that we have lost
widens her eyes:
she is one with painter and poet.

Phoebe Hesketh

PABLO PICASSO, *Child Holding a Dove*, 1901, The National Gallery (London), oil on canvas, 73 × 54 cm

— *Child with Dove* —

There is a picture on our wall,
A girl in blue, a coloured ball,
A sideways-leaning gentle face,
A pigeon held in soft embrace.

I like her downward-pointed toes,
The ease with which he paints her nose;
I'm just content to look and think;
I can't say what I mean in ink.

And why should teacher, fingers spread,
Feeling for words behind his head,
Say, with a face almost in pain,
Of this Picasso man in Spain
How all his life he's sought a way
Of saying what I want to say?

For even a child can plainly see
He does his drawings just like me.

Gregory Harrison

41

PABLO PICASSO, *The Three Musicians*, 1921, The Museum of Modern Art (New York), oil on canvas, 200 × 222 cm

— *The Three Musicians* —

Caramel sweet the clarinet sound
sings to the harlequin man
with the sharp yellow guitar.

The mystery man picks up
the riff on his accordion,
fingers squeezing out

black on white notes,
red hot and cool blue.

Flat as card,
round sound.

Valerie Bird

— *Olé* —

This is the picture of we three,
The Maestro, Carlos and me,
when we all dressed up
in Pablo's wardrobe for a trip
to Dreamland. Can't you just hear
the music as if you were there
with its squeezebox of notes
at full stretch, the clarinet's
chalumeau tootle*, the gold guitar,   *low reedy note*
and our six feet thumping the floor,
olé, and Conchita's making eight
as she brought us each a heaped plate
of steaming paella. Oh it was great
with Pablo urging us on – *More! More!* –
until the neighbours hammered at the door
and we let them in. Then we all took bets
on how many days and nights
we could keep it up, this being without a care
in the world, this wish-you-were-here
rumpus of happiness, this non-stop
once-in-a-lifetime letting-rip
of The Maestro, Carlos and me
in Pablo's picture of we three.

John Mole

Portrait of Titus

HERMENSZ VAN RIJN REMBRANDT, *Portrait of Titus*, c.1657, The Wallace Collection (London), oil on canvas, 70.8 × 58.4 cm

— *To Titus, Rembrandt's son* —

I remembered you as younger –
   sevenish – for thirty years
misremembered a fair child
   painted with such tenderness

love hung in the space between
   your image and its looker-on.
Tears welled in my eyes. I thought:
   How the father loves his son,

motherless and delicate;
   how he wishes to preserve
infancy from adult state:
   coarsened, burdened, hairy, grave.

Can it be that you who were
   a child three centuries ago,
grow up slowly in your frame?
   Now I see you as fourteen,

almost turned into a man,
   and observe a hint of down
shading upper lip and chin;
   see, between your brows, a frown,

faint, as yet, but questioning.
   'Father, how long must I stay
dressed up ready to go out?
   Father, Hannah waits for me.'

Titus wears his scarlet hat
   and his pendant, on gold chain.
'Father, life's too short to wait
   till I am old. I must be gone.'

Rembrandt paints as if he must
   save from time the restless youth
never to become time's jest:
   old-agedness. His love paints truth.

Anna Adams

STANLEY SPENCER, *A Village in Heaven*, 1937, Manchester City Art Galleries, oil on canvas, 43.5 × 183.5 cm

— *Stanley Spencer's* A Village in Heaven —

What is possessing
   These women, these children,
      Bouncing, ballooning,
Lazing and loving,
   Shamelessly, aimlessly
      Outside the Park?

If this is Paradise
   Some of the blessed ones,
      Straw-hatted schoolgirls,
Goggling schoolboys
   Seem to be leaving
      In some disorder.

By the Memorial
   (The shell-shocked Memorial)
      A solid stone preacher
Bawls out accusingly
   Someone quite daring
      In black silk pyjamas.

Where are the men?
    Are they stilled on some battlefield,
        Silent, undead?
Was it for them
    That these few Flanders' poppies
        Loyally bled?

Whose is the Great House
    (There must be a Great House)
        Beyond the trim wall?
Is it a figure
    Of love or of terror,
        Or no-one at all?

There goes the painter
    (The pudding-hat painter)
        Turning his back
On the women, the children,
    Keeping his answers
        Tight-close to his chest.
        But perhaps that is best.

Charles Causley

MARIANNE STOKES, *Polishing Pans*, 1887, Walker Art Gallery (Liverpool), oil on canvas, 59 × 79.3 cm

— *Polishing Pans* —

She rubs and rubs till her hands are sore
and dirt from the pans stains her face grey
and her dress must be black because of the grime
and she's weary of working downstairs, alone.
Ten or eleven I'd guess is her age
and always the tang of copper and brass
pollutes her hair, her skin and her breath.

Is she cook's skivvy, the scullery-maid,
lowliest servant in some stately home?
What are her dreams as she sits in the gloom
and forces each pan to glisten and gleam?
Does anyone say she's done her work well
and send her out to play in the sun?

Peggy Poole

ALFRED WALLIS, *Penzance Harbour*, c. 1935, Kettle's Yard, University of Cambridge, ship's paint on cardboard, 30.5 × 45.5 cm

Alfred Wallis Day-Dreams in the Bath

West-south-west of my big toe,
Past wreckers' lights and smugglers' caves,
Where murky waters heave and flow,
A trawler bobs upon the waves.

On board, I paint on board or wood
Of what I know, not what I see.
I paint what I have understood –
The ships, the winds, the Cornish sea.

The picture in my mind's eye frames
That sea as grey as wet cement,
With paper boats from children's games;
One navigates a gradient!

St. Michael's Mount* drops in and sticks,
A fly in the impasto* caught;
Meanwhile my brush plays other tricks –
Martello* floats by lost in thought!

The harbour light to starboard leans
And beams benignly from the quay,
Politely asks what all this means
For Cornwall's local geography.

The town's reply is snatched away –
The breeze is up, the seagulls scream.
The picture fades; no toe today
Can steer me through this bath-time dream.

*top right
*thickly applied paint

*a small circular tower for coastal defence

Michael Benton

The Harbour Wall

In winter,
when chill winds blow,
and the sea is white-grey
as an icy puddle,
the harbour wall
curves its long stone arm
around the fishing boats
bob-bobbing in a huddle.
'I'll keep you safe
from winter's storms,'
the wall seems to say
as it gives the boats a cuddle.

Wes Magee

PAOLO UCCELLO, *A Hunt in a Forest*, c.1465, Ashmolean Museum, University of Oxford, oil on wood, 73.5 × 177 cm

Paolo (Uccello) would sit up all night working out his complicated perspective systems, and when his wife called him to come to bed, the artist would reply 'O what a delightful thing perspective is!'

— *Perspectives* —

Sit here, child,
Held safe before me,
High on the saddlebow of my horse,
And on your mind's eye, imprint the scene.

You will remember this.

Mark how, beneath the vault of slender trees that arch their tracery
Against a darkening sky, the nearest horsemen check their flight,

And Mario, cloak flying, spurs to outflank the little herd
Of bounding roebuck whose hooves drum lightly on the forest floor.

Look how they leap to evade the elegant, deadly jaws, so tireless in pursuit
Which harry their nimble quarry towards the receding gloom.

We have them now, between the lancing river and the dogs.

See how the pent hounds bark and strain to join their brothers in the pack
And launch their anxious bodies in the chase.

Just so their masters, intent upon their task, in scarlet, gold and blue,
Daggers at their belts and steel tipped spears in hand,

Hurry towards the darkness over jewelled turf
Embroidered with a thousand flowers.

Such richness you are heir to!

Do not forget; hold one thought fast:
So it is now; so it will always be.
Our forests march on to
infinity.

Peter Benton

JAMES ABBOTT McNEILL WHISTLER, *Miss Cicely Alexander: Harmony in Grey and Green*, 1872, The Tate Gallery (London), canvas, 190 × 98 cm

— Best Friends —

My best friend is Faroukh.
He has a holy toe nail on a chain
and when he laughs his teeth are shiny.
But last week he told on me
when I was making faces in PE

so my best friend is Julia.
She runs as fast as Miss Delaney.
She smells of flowers and sherbet lemons
and made me a sun hat for my rabbit.
But Delroy called me sissy

so my best friend is Alec.
He knows a very rude word,
and how to tie an everlasting knot.
But he likes fighting best, and I have
nine bruises from his karate chops

so my best friend is Cicely.
We sing together, make up riddles
when she climbs down from her frame after
   dark.
Her magic hat makes us invisible.
She never minds playing my games.

Carole Satyamurti

— Miss Cicely Alexander —

To you, I suppose, I look sweet and demure,
Here in this solemn room of green and grey –
But inside I'm raging, I hate *everybody*!

You see, I was out in the fields on my pony,
Jumping the brushwood I'd heaped up this morning,
The wind was whipping my cheeks and my fingers,
The dirt flying up under galloping hoofbeats,
As I urged my steed onwards and up! and over,
Thorns tearing my clothes as we dashed past the hedges,
And the sun and the air and all the birds singing –

Then suddenly 'Cicely! Time for your sitting!'
'Sitting' they call it, and I have to stand
For hours with my back straight and my legs aching,
My hair pinned back and fluffed out and tickling,
And my frock and hat pulled and tweaked into position,
And it's 'Put your left foot just a bit further forward,
Now turn out the toe. And Cicely, dear,
Do try to smile!' So much do I long
To be out in the meadow
That look! A few daisies have followed me here
And two little butterflies.

Heather Harvey

— Growing Pains —

I've been standing here for *ages* in this
stupid dress, one foot poked out as if
it's heading forward while the other's stuck.

If only I could skip out to the haymaking
and slide down the stack in my simple slip,
or just get on with reading *Through the Looking-glass.*

Can you tell what I'm thinking from my face?
This artist's creepy and I feel he's prying
right into my mind through spying-glasses*.

I'd like to burst out of the place like Alice.
Next thing they'll have me laced in stays. I'll faint.
What Mad Hatter made this hat I have to pose with?

Sometimes I dream that in some future time
girls will finally be free of all these trappings.
Papa guffaws: 'She'll even want the *vote** next!'

Sylvia Kantaris

*Lewis Carroll's book was published in 1872, the date of the painting

*See page 76

*The Suffragette (Votes for Women) Movement started only a generation later

DIEGO RODRIGUEZ DE SILVA Y VELASQUEZ, *Prince Baltasar Carlos in Silver*, 1633, The Wallace Collection (London), oil on canvas, 117.8 × 95.9 cm

Prince Baltasar Carlos in Silver, *by Velasquez, and* Miss Cicely Alexander, *by Whistler*

BOTH: Like butterflies in boxes, fixed by art
           in timelessness, dressed up in finery,
           we're both enraged, and soon the tears will start.

BALTASAR: Across the centuries, heart cries to heart:
           I'm not a Silver-washed Fritillary;
           I am a living boy, transfixed by art.

CICELY: I won't be looked on as a Cabbage White:
           hot blood flows under snowy drapery.
           I'm so fed up that soon the tears will start.

BOTH: We are not ornaments for looking at:
           White Admiral nor Painted Peacock-fly;
           Poor butterflies in boxes, fixed by art,

           long to be ragged gypsies with bare feet
           and dancing wild in hoyden* liberty: *inelegant
           we're both enraged and soon the tears will start.

CICELY: I'll shred my petticoats, I'll squash my hat;
BALTASAR: I'll draw my sword and make them set me free.
BOTH: Like butterflies in boxes, fixed by art,
           we're both enraged and soon the tears will start.

Anna Adams

JOSEPH WRIGHT OF DERBY, *An Experiment on a Bird in the Air-Pump*, 1768, The National Gallery (London), oil on canvas, 182.9 × 243.9 cm

Experiment with an Air-Pump

('There is a valve on top of the glass bowl. When the valve is sealed and the air pumped out, the bird collapses from lack of oxygen. This reaction may seem obvious to us, but it was new knowledge to many people in the mid-18th century, who wanted scientific proof.'   Robert Cumming)

I withdraw to the shadows, seeking air –
The heat of bodies, and that pickled skull,
A grotesque fondue*, cooking in candlelight,   *meat cooked in hot oil
Enough to turn the stomach.
              He eyes me still,
This wizard, holds my gaze, conspiring now
To draw me in to arbitrate* on death.   *decide
'Well, sir,' he gestures, 'shall I close the valve?'
The room distorts, as seen through concave glass,
As if inside a bell-jar I am trapped.
The others' glances criss-cross in the air;
I read each mind's reaction in its gaze:
The thinker weighing death in wisdom's scales;

The fearful girls, their reasonable dad;
The man who measures life to its last gasp;
The youth who reckons nothing but the view;
The lovers lost within a world elsewhere.
Each gaze is solo, separate, alone.
'Well, sir?'
            I shake my head. 'Let down the cage.'
His look untroubled, innocent as light,
The boy obeys. A pinioned* life, perhaps.   *with clipped wings
But if we cannot all live free as birds
To chase the moonlight round the curve of space,
We can at least make sure we get some air.

Michael Benton

GALLERY

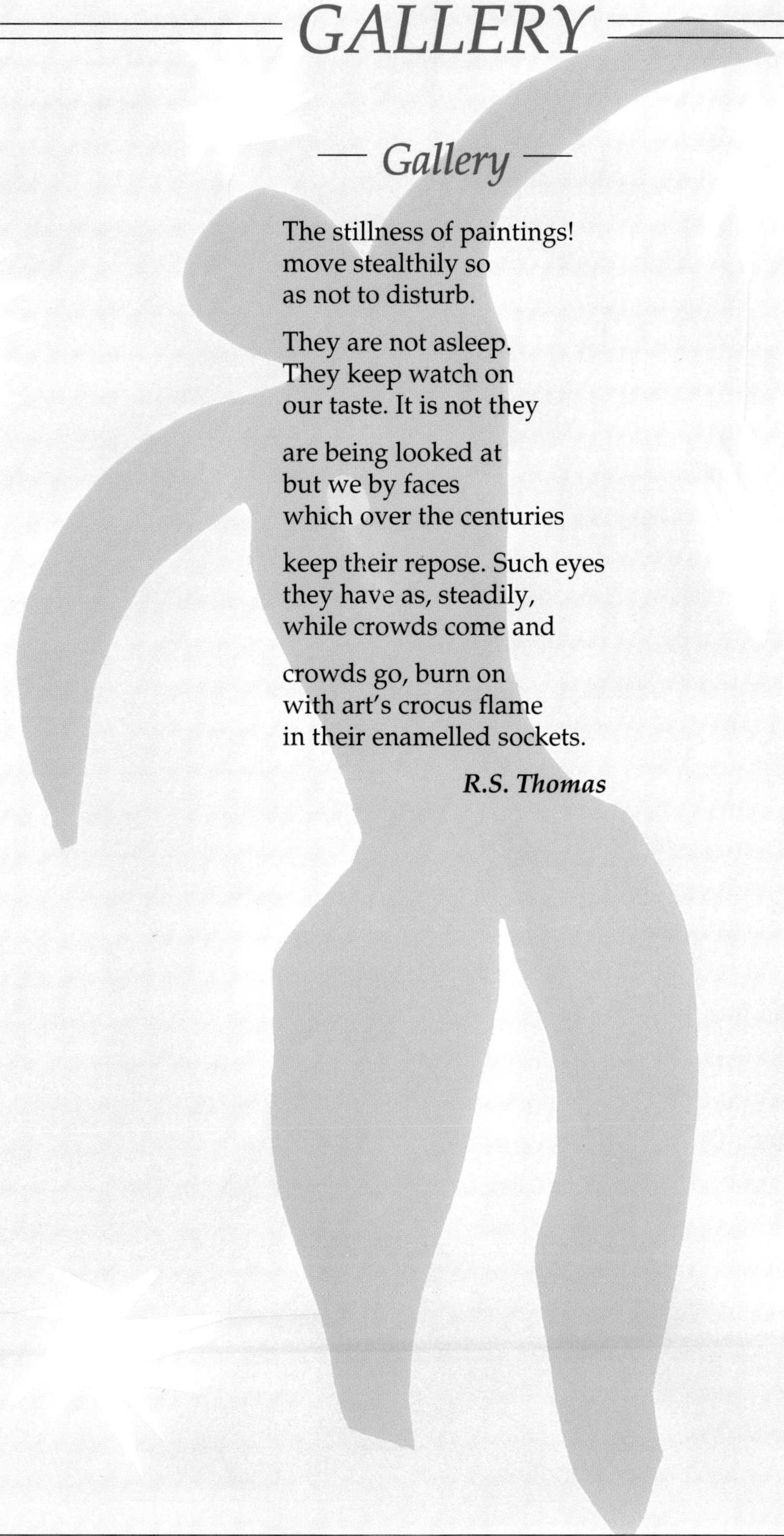

— *Gallery* —

The stillness of paintings!
move stealthily so
as not to disturb.

They are not asleep.
They keep watch on
our taste. It is not they

are being looked at
but we by faces
which over the centuries

keep their repose. Such eyes
they have as, steadily,
while crowds come and

crowds go, burn on
with art's crocus flame
in their enamelled sockets.

R.S. Thomas

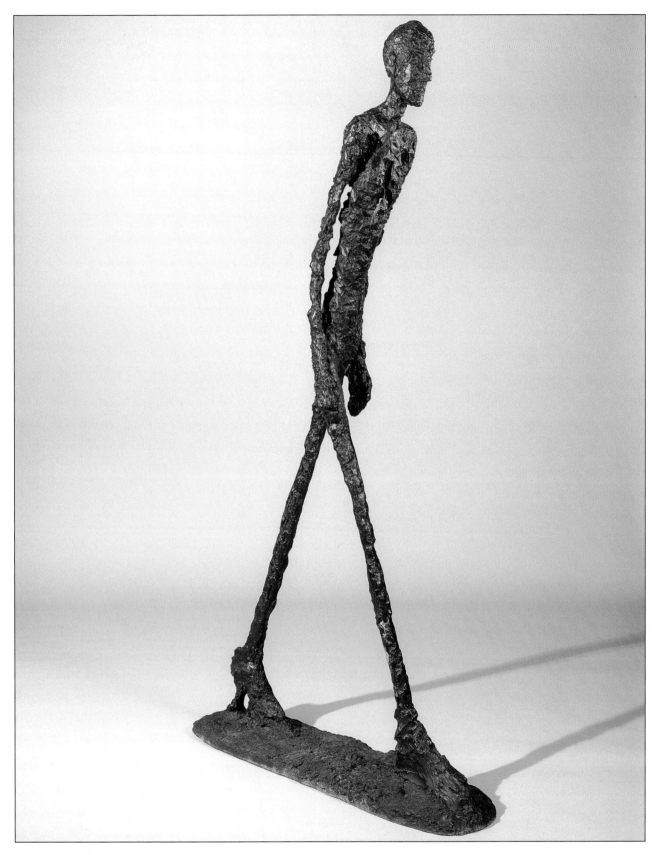

ALBERTO GIACOMETTI, *L'homme Qui Marche (Walking Man)*, Louisiana Museum of Modern Art, (Denmark), bronze, 192 cm

GIUSEPPE ARCIMBOLDO, *Water*, c.1570, Kunsthistorisches Museum (Vienna), oil on canvas, 66.5 × 50.5 cm

KATSUSHIKA HOKUSAI, *The Great Wave*, 1831, Victoria & Albert Museum (London), colour wood block print, 25 × 37.1 cm

ANDREW WYETH, *Christina's World*, 1948, Museum of Modern Art (New York), tempera on gessoed panel, 81.9 × 121.3 cm

HENRI MATISSE, *Flight of Icarus*, 1947, Ecole des Beaux arts, Paris, gouache stencil, 42 × 32.5 cm

F.N. SOUZA, *Crucifixion*, 1959, The Tate Gallery (London), oil on board, 182.9 × 101.6 cm

JASPER JOHNS, *Zero Through Nine*, 1961, The Tate Gallery (London), oil on canvas, 137.2 × 104.8 cm

MAKING CONNECTIONS

— Painter and Poet —

Watch the painter, children.
The painter is painting himself.
Palette enfisted, aloft; brush brandished.
There are men watching the painter painting,
Children. The spectacled one with a beard
Is saying *Magnificent! a touch of sfumato* there!*   *light and shade blending
                                                      without borders, like smoke.

O, a very good investment, gentleman. You can't go wrong,
Financially speaking, when the artist has used
So much technique. There! did you see how he stippled?
My advice is, certainly purchase. Always a market
For work of this kind. The painter listens, children,
And smiles a banker's smile. He does
A spot more impasting.*   *applying paint thickly

Now, children, the poet. He is less exciting.
All he brandishes is a ball-point,
Which he plays with on unastonishing paper.
See him unload his disorganised wordhoard,
Children, as he sits alone. No one comes
To admire, or commission. Having only
Himself to please, he tinkers at pleasing himself.
Watch silently now as that metaphor
Fans slowly out, like a fin from the sea.
Did you notice him then, secret and shy as an otter,
Transferring an epithet?* See that artless adverb   *adjective
Mutate into a pun! And now – O children,
Keep very quiet – he is inserting a verb!
A cryptic cipher*, for friends' eyes only, he splices   *secret code
Into his work, not guessing that what he writes
Will turn into a *text*, a *set text*,
Children; nor that you will think
He committed it deliberately to hurt you.

Invest in the painter, children; as for the poet,
Bad luck is catching. I should steer clear.

U.A. Fanthorpe

Introduction

This section is addressed to the pupils but the teacher will want to read through the suggestions and discuss the activities with them before they begin. We have not attempted to cover every painting or poem, but to give a wide range of activities, many of which can be applied easily to other paintings and poems.

The suggestions for classroom activities are split into two sections:

I Teaching ideas for specific poems and paintings, most of which can be completed within a double lesson and a homework;

II A brief outline of general themes or projects suitable for more extended work.

I Teaching Ideas

Brueghel: *Landscape with the Fall of Icarus*
Gareth Owen and Dannie Abse (pp 12–15)

In Greek mythology, Daedalus was a craftsman and inventor who built wings made out of wax and feathers for himself and his son Icarus. He intended to use them to escape from Greece which was under the rule of King Minos. Icarus, however, disobeyed his father and flew too close to the sun. The wax melted and he fell to his death.

● Look carefully at Brueghel's painting. Notice how the diagonal lines draw our attention to the lower right-hand corner where Icarus disappears beneath the waves. How do the other figures react to the fall?

Both poems imagine the moments before Icarus hits the water. Gareth Owen's poem follows Icarus's conversation with Daedalus on a mobile telephone while Dannie Abse's poem describes Icarus's thoughts as he plunges towards earth.

Prepared readings

● Gareth Owen's poem needs a single voice. Rehearse the conversation in detail:
  – Where do you need to speed up and slow down?
  – Are there to be any pauses?
  – Will the tone of your voice change?

You may be able to dramatise the performance by holding a mobile telephone and somebody miming Daedalus talking on his telephone.

● A reading of Dannie Abse's poem could mix Icarus's voice with that of a chorus. The chorus might speak 'A little to the left ... and now' from verse 3 and 'show me your face ... Launch a boat', verse 4.

Dali: *Metamorphosis of Narcissus*
Heather Harvey and Moniza Alvi (pp 16–17)

> In the ancient myth . . . Narcissus is a youth of great beauty: 'Many lads and many girls fell in love with him but his soft young body housed a pride so unyielding that none of those boys and girls dared to touch him.' Eventually, a nymph named Echo fell in love with him. When he rejected her she pined away until only her voice was left. Hearing the complaints of his rejected lovers, the goddess of vengeance, Nemesis, punished Narcissus by arranging for him to experience for himself the pain of unrequited love. Since he could only love himself, she caused him to see his reflection in a pool of water. Narcissus fell in love, but was unable to embrace the beautiful stranger in the pool. Frustrated, Narcissus in turn pined away and finally died. At his death the goddess relented slightly and transformed him into the flower that we know as the Narcissus.
>
> Dali shows us first of all Narcissus as he was in life, posing 'narcissistically' on a pedestal in the background, gazing down admiringly at himself. Then we see him kneeling in the fatal pool in the process of transformation into the strange hand holding an egg from which springs the new Narcissus flower.
>
> (Simon Wilson, *The Tate Gallery; An Illustrated Companion*, 1989, p 163)

Salvador Dali's painting shows this metamorphosis. Like many of his pictures, it attempts to make unreal, dreamlike sequences seem real by using a highly finished, almost shiny, technique. Objects take on several meanings or identities, as here where Narcissus can be read as either a figure or a rock formation.

- Hear the two poems read aloud and notice all the details that each of the writers has included.

Individual writing

- Study the picture again, particularly the figure of Narcissus, his reflection in the pool, and the strange hand in the foreground.
- Write your own poem or story about Narcissus's transformation. You could write it from the viewpoint of either Echo or Nemesis. Look again at Simon Wilson's extract above to help you:
  - What might they say?
  - How would they speak?

 Degas: *Woman Ironing*
U.A. Fanthorpe (pp 22–23)

Drama

U.A. Fanthorpe's poem about Degas' painting is a dialogue between painter and sitter.

With a few simple props and some rehearsal, the poem can be presented like a scene from a play.

- In groups of three, decide on the following:
  voices:
  – a boy's voice for the words spoken by the painter in verses 3 and 5
  – a girl's voice for the spoken words in verse 4
  – another girl's voice for the narrator in the rest of the poem.
  characters:
  – the mood and tone of voice of each of the three characters.
  props:
  – make a list of all the things you need. Then discuss whether you can get them. You will probably have to improvise.
  movements:
  – how are you going to position yourselves? Where are the ironing board and easel going to be ? Should the narrator move around? Draw a sketch of what you decide.

- Discuss these points and any other ideas you have, rehearse your scene and present it to the class.

 Escher: *Drawing Hands*   Anon: *Vase/Faces*
Heather Harvey (p 24)   Colin Rowbotham (p 25)

In Pairs

- Look carefully at Escher's picture of *Drawing Hands*.
  Try to decide what is going on:
  – Which hand is drawing which?
  – Does the drawing have a beginning and an end?
  – Can the hands ever finish their task?

- Listen to Heather Harvey's poem read aloud. It is a special kind of verse called a Pantoum in which certain lines are repeated in a set order.

  Can you work it out? You will need to give each line a letter or colour and join the repetitions with arrows like this:

Again your hand begins to draw	a
I feel my fingers live and warm	b
We sketch and shade the wrists, and more,	c
As each of each creates the form.	d
I feel my fingers live and warm	b

(You will find that ten sentences are repeated so you will need to label the lines from **a** to **j** or find ten different colours.)

The second line of the first verse becomes the first line of the second verse and the last line of the first verse becomes the third line of the second verse . . . and so on. Something else happens to the first line. What is it?

- Look at the *Vase/Face* picture. What happens as you stare at it?
- Listen to Colin Rowbotham's Pantoum about this picture.

Group Reading

- In groups of about five, choose one of the Pantoums and share out the lines.

  Practise reading it taking each voice in turn. Do your best to create a seamless reading.

Writing

- Write a group Pantoum about one of the illusion pictures below.

Can you see a young woman and an old woman?

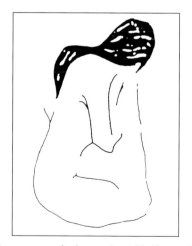

Can you see a fat face and a girl half-turned away?

 Antony Gormley: *Field*
Gillian Clarke and Peggy Poole (pp 26–27)

All the figures are moulded by hand. Each one is between 8 cm and 26 cm tall.

Field is a sculpture of tiny figures made out of clay. Each figure is moulded by hand by a group of people working with the artist. Then it is installed in a gallery. The sculpture varies according to where it is installed; there has been an *American Field*, a *European Field* and a *Field for the British Isles*. It takes the staff several days to set out the figures on the floor under Antony Gormley's direction. The gallery staff say that they are sure the figures move about at night!

- Look carefully at the sculpture. Imagine that you are in the gallery. Think about this crowd in front of you.
  Jot down your thoughts in the way suggested below.

Mapping your responses

- Make a sketch of the sculpture and copy out Gillian Clarke's poem. Sketching and copying can help you to remember details and to understand the ideas.
- Add your own notes around the sketch and the poem (use a different coloured pen for this). You will soon have lots of ideas about what the sculpture and poem mean to you. Here are some suggestions to get you started:

Clay and human beings linked to each other.

European Field

– an installation by Antony Gormley

Repeated, insistent numbers: the pressure of the words is like the pressure of all those faces.

Thirty-five thousand faces in a field
the colour of clay and flesh and blood
crammed between clean white walls of a gallery.
Thirty-five thousand on tip-toe
craning their necks
breathing like a field of corn.

Thirty-five thousand voices asking
why, why, why
like wind in the grasses
of graveyards and old battlefields.
Seventy-thousand ears listening
to no answer.

1st field is the gallery, crammed, oppressive, tense because there is no answer.

We have paid to see them.
We did not expect to be stared at,
or that they would move in to live with us,
taking root in the field of our minds,
whispering all night
'we are you, you, you.'

Thirty-five thousand figures
crumbling in my head
to bones and dust and ashes
under a field of flowering grasses.

2nd field is the poet's mind, taken over by this army of occupation.

Galleries
should carry a health warning.

Gillian Clarke

Why this humorous ending?

Figures break up into the earth from which they came; the flowering grasses seem like their memorial.

Space – how do the figures fill the space? How do they relate to each other, to the gallery walls, floor and doors?

Gaze – their 'eyes' or rather eye sockets mostly look ahead. Gormley calls the ones at the front 'star gazers' as they look up. Are they pleading or questioning?

Size – the figures are no more than 26 cm high. Would a small child and an adult see them differently?

Material – what are they made of and who made them?

Mood – how do they make you feel? Are they sad, happy, humorous, threatening?

Characters – how do you read their expressions? Are they all the same?

In groups

● When you have jotted down your ideas, compare your notes with two or three others.
  – Were your reactions to the sculpture similar?
  – How do your feelings about the sculpture compare with Gillian Clarke's?

● Read Peggy Poole's poem about the sculpture. How does her 'reading' compare with Gillian Clarke's and your own?

● Looking at photographs of the sculpture is not the same as looking at the original. Simon (aged 10) and Sophie (aged 12) saw *Field for The British Isles* at the Hayward Gallery, London. Here are some of their comments. See how they compare with your ideas.

SIMON: It's weird. How many are there?

SOPHIE: They're not all the same. It'd be boring if they were.

SIMON: Look, there's patterns in the clay, different colours.

SOPHIE: That's to show different cultures, different countries.

SIMON: There's fat ones, thin ones, little ones, . . . they're a clay people. A lot of helpless little people.

SOPHIE: It's like they're trapped in here in a big cold world, waiting to see what happens next.

SIMON: They're all looking at us, not at each other, a whole army looking at us. What do you think they want?

SOPHIE: They've only got eyes. It'd be different if they had mouths or ears – they'd just look, well, like this (*draws two simple circles, one with a smiling mouth, the other with a downturned mouth*); but eyes are dominant. You can do everything with eyes: you can see . . . smell food and see it . . . . and you can show everything, you communicate with your eyes. They look sad.

SIMON: They're people of clay, like we're made of earth ... they're all squashed in.

SOPHIE: They're like us, a whole community but different individuals as well. There's a field for America and a field for Europe, that's because we are all basically the same but in some ways different.

Kandinsky: *Swinging*
Moniza Alvi and Heather Harvey (pp 34–35)

- Before reading the poems, look carefully at the picture and jot down some notes about all the things that it suggests to you.
  - what might the circles be?
  - or the multi-coloured patch of squares?
  - the two white-tipped shapes?
  - or the blue, curving shapes?

  Perhaps you get the feeling that the whole picture is of a landscape, or a city, or a person's head or, given the title, perhaps it suggests music or even a band?

Group Reading

- In groups talk about your different ideas and then read the two poems. Moniza Alvi's poem can be shared between two voices, with the painter coming in at the end. Heather Harvey's poem goes round the picture, fixing on one detail after another every line and a bit. Read it aloud, handing on to the next voice as each new idea is introduced.

Individual/Pair writing

- Use your notes to write your own poem.

  Take the opening lines of Moniza Alvi's poem and then continue with your own idea of what the picture is about.

  Or try writing a 'round', following the model of Heather Harvey's poem.

If you decide to try this:
- first make a list of the shapes in the order that they will come in your poem;
- then look at each shape carefully and write down three or four words, or a phrase, or a comparison that the shape suggests;
- now link them up with a single word, as Heather Harvey has done, or in some other way.

Magritte: *Time Transfixed*
Carol Ann Duffy, Carole Satyamurti, Heather Harvey (pp 36–38)
Magritte: *Golconda*
Peter Benton (p 39)

Margritte was perhaps the most poetic of what are called the surrealist painters. Like poets they put images side by side in unexpected ways so that they spark off unexpected ideas in our minds. Magritte would never explain his paintings: they are what we make of them.

In *Time Transfixed*, as in a dream, a steam train rushes out of the fireplace of an ordinary house. A solid clock stands on the mantelpiece beneath a mirror.

In *Golconda* men in bowler hats float up into the air above the city streets.

- Look carefully at the two paintings for a few minutes. Then pick one and jot down any ideas or associations, however strange, or absurd they may be. Talk about your ideas in pairs or groups.
- Listen to the three poems about *Time Transfixed*.

   (For Carole Satyamurti, the clock suggests a leaving present given to mark a man's retirement. The clock in the Thinking Room in Carol Ann Duffy's poem is also a clock in a Waiting Room. Heather Harvey's poem suggests other dream-like images for time standing still which are as strange as the ones in the painting.)

Writing

- Discuss the poems and then write your own poem called *Time Transfixed*.

   If you are looking for a place to start, think about what might have happened just before or just after the moment of the painting.
   – For instance, you could write your poem from the point of view of the engine driver or someone sitting in the room.
   – Or you could use Heather Harvey's verses as a model for your own poem, and pattern your verse in the same way that she has:

Time will stand still
When ....
....
And ....
....

You could build a class poem of several verses this way.

   When Peter Benton looked at *Golconda*, he found himself asking lots of questions:
   – were the men in bowler hats going up or down?
   – who and what were they?
   – why did they all look like little versions of Magritte in their bowler hats and overcoats?

You may see them quite differently.

- If you do, write a poem saying who you think they are.

Time Transfixed and *Golconda* put ordinary things into unexpected places and by relating them, create a strange dream-like effect.

- Can you think of other places where this surreal style is used?
  Pop videos, television adverts, magazine adverts, computer games and CD inserts should all provide examples.

- Create your own surreal scene. You could imagine, illustrate or write about a dream landscape or a dream room. You might like to use a 'surreal image generator' to get you started. Just link the ideas below randomly together.

Imagine:

a computer	crawling with ants	on a beach
a tree	on fire	in a wardrobe
a cloud	balanced on a rock	in a coffin
a supermarket trolley	hanging in mid-air	under a full moon

Add your own images.

 Whistler: *Miss Cicely Alexander*
Anna Adams, Carole Satyamurti, Sylvia Kantaris and Heather Harvey (pp 52–53)

- Before reading any of the poems look carefully at the picture and jot down your first impressions of Miss Cicely Alexander. You could think about:
  – the way she is dressed;
  – the way she stands;
  – her expression;
  – the background against which she is painted.
- Now jot down what thoughts might be passing through her mind.

Writing

- Write a poem about the painting. Use your notes to help you.
  You will find it helpful if you decide which point of view you are writing from:
  – is it about what you see and feel when you look at the painting?
  – is it what you imagine Miss Cicely Alexander to be thinking as she is painted?
  – is it about what the artist is thinking as he paints?
  – is it about the reaction of Cicely's wealthy parents when they see the painting?
  – or are you going to choose another view?

Now, enjoy the poems.

Group Reading

- In pairs or groups, choose a poem and practise reading it to decide how it sounds best. Anna Adams's poem on p 55 is a conversation between Cicely and the young Prince Baltasar Carlos, from the painting by Velasquez. You will need two voices for this.

    (Prince Baltasar was destined to be King of Spain but he died when he was seventeen.)
- Share your readings and your own poems.
    - Talk about the character each writer gives to Cicely and the character that some of you may have given her in your poems. Sylvia Kantaris writes about her poem:

    'I discovered that *Through the Looking Glass* was published in the same year as Whistler portrayed Miss Cicely whom I see as some kind of pouting Alice.'
    - What different points of view do you find?
- Look at Tenniel's drawing of Alice. It is a deliberate copy of the girl in Millais's *My First Sermon*. With Whistler's picture, you now have three versions of Victorian girlhood – at home, in a railway carriage, in church. Imagine her somewhere else, sketch the scene and write about her.

JOHN EVERETT MILLAIS, *My First Sermon*, 1863, Guildhall Art Gallery (London), oil on canvas, 92 × 76.8 cm

One of the original illustrations of Alice by JOHN TENNIEL

II *Themes and Projects*

1 Making your own anthology

Either individually, in pairs or as a class, collect postcards of your favourite paintings. You will find lots of these on sale at art gallery and museum shops, at bookshops and at card and poster shops. Write your own poems to accompany them and present your anthology as a book or a wall display. If you use a word processor you can make your work look very professional.

2 Posters

Make a 'poster wall' in your classroom or along a stretch of corridor by displaying large-scale reproductions of paintings. First write to the main London galleries (addresses on pp 79–80) to find out what is available. Explore your local galleries and bookshops too. Your school art department may be able to help. Don't forget other sources such as 'art' calendars which are out of date within a year. The reproductions on these can be of very good quality. Gradually the class can build up a collection.

On your poster wall you might be able to feature a single artist one month and a group of artists another. You may want to explore other areas not covered in this book, for example African, Caribbean, Mexican, Indian or Japanese art. Whatever your choice, put brief notes about the artists, any information you can find about the painting and, of course, your own writing and poems in response to the pictures.

3 Tape/slide presentation

Put together a sequence of poems and paintings that you like as a tape/slide programme for a particular audience – maybe for pupils in another group or for an assembly. Think carefully about the theme or focus your programme will have. You can then write a script to link your paintings and poems and, of course, you can include some of your own poems too.

The easiest way of getting hold of slides is to buy them from the galleries at around 50p each, but you may also find that your school art department has a set and there are loan sets available from some public libraries.

4 Storytelling

Some say that every picture tells a story and it is true that every picture in this book has either a story embedded within it or one that could be invented about it. Choose a painting that appeals to you from here or from somewhere else and develop a story around it, either through discussion or through writing.

5 Gallery visit: making a Pupils' Guide

Visit your nearest art gallery or one of the main city art galleries. Find two or three paintings that really appeal to you. Find out as much as you can about your choices. Buy a postcard or find a reproduction of the painting to help you remember the details.

Write a short account of your choices, including all the information you have discovered and the reasons why you like the paintings. If everyone in the group does this, you could put the pages together into a *Pupils' Guide* for others to use. (Don't forget that galleries often have an education officer who will generally be only too happy to help you, particularly if given sufficient notice of your visit.)

6 'Desert island' paintings

Which six paintings would you choose to have with you on a desert island? Don't just confine yourself to our selection in this book; browse through other books in your local or school library.

Compare lists and see if there are painters or paintings that are particularly popular.

If you could have just one painting on your island, which would it be? Write about the feelings and thoughts this painting gives you, either as a prose description or as a poem.

= GALLERY INFORMATION =

For a full list see *Museums and Galleries in Great Britain and Ireland* (ABC Historic Publications). Times of opening are Monday–Saturday (Sunday). For bank holidays and festivals, visitors are advised to check opening times in advance. STD codes given are from London.

Aberdeen
Art Gallery and Museums, Schoolhill. 10–5; Thu 10–8 (2–5). Tel: 01224 646333
Belfast
Ulster Museum, Botanic Gardens BT9 5AB. Mon–Fri 10–4.50; Sat 1–4.50 (2–4.50). 01232 383000
Birmingham
City Museum and Art Gallery, Chamberlain Square B3 3DH. 10–5 (12.30–5). Tel: 0121 2352834
Barber Institute of Fine Arts. The University B15 2TS. 10–5; (2–5). Tel: 0121 4147333
Bristol
City of Bristol Museum and Art Gallery, Queen's Road BS8 1RL. 10–5 (10–5). Tel: 0117 9223571
Cambridge
Fitzwilliam Museum, Trumpington Street. Tues–Sat 10–5 (2.15–5). Tel: 01223 332900
Cardiff
National Museum of Wales. Tues–Sun 10–5. Tel: 01222 397951
Dublin
National Gallery of Ireland, Merrion Square, West 2. 10–5.30; Thu 10–8.30 (2–5).
Tel: 00353 16615133
Edinburgh
National Gallery of Scotland, The Mound EH2 2EL. 10–5 (2–5). Tel: 0131 5568921
Scottish National Gallery of Modern Art, Belford Road EH4 3DR. 10–5 (2–5). Tel: 0131 5568921
Scottish National Portrait Gallery, Queen Street EH2 1JD. 10–5 (2–5). Tel: 0131 5568921
Glasgow
Art Gallery and Museum, Kelvingrove. 10–5 (11–5). Tel: 0141 2872700
Burrel Collection, 2060 Pollokshaws Road G43 1AT. 10–5 (2–5). Closed on Tuesdays until further notice. Tel: 0141 6497151
Hunterian Art Gallery, 82 Hillhead Street. 9.30–5; Closed Sundays. Tel: 0141 3398855 ext. 7431
Pollok House, 2060 Pollokshaws Road. 10–5 (2–5). Closed part of the year. Tel: 0141 6497547
Hull
Ferens Art Gallery, Queen Victoria Square. 10–5 (1.30–4.30). Tel: 01482 613902
Leeds
City Art Gallery. Mon–Sat 10–5 (late night opening, Wed until 8pm); (1–5). Tel: 0113 2478248
Henry Moore Centre for the Study of Sculpture. Mon–Sun 10–5.30 (open until 9pm on Wednesday). Tel: 0113 2469469
Liverpool
Walker Art Gallery, William Brown Street L3 8EL. 10–5 (2–5). Tel: 0151 2070001
Sudley Art Gallery, Mossley Hill Road. 10–5 (12–5). Tel: 0151 7243245
Lady Lever Art Gallery, Port Sunlight. 10–5 (12–5). Tel: 0151 6453623
Tate Gallery Liverpool, Albert Dock L3 4BB. Tues–Sun 10–6. Tel: 0151 7093223
Manchester
City Art Gallery, Mosley Street. Mon 11–5.30, Tues–Sat 10–5.30 (2–5.30). Tel: 0161 2365244
Whitworth Art Gallery, University of Manchester, Oxford Road. 10–5 (2–5) Tel. 0161 2757452
Newcastle upon Tyne
Laing Art Gallery, Higham Place. 10–5; (2–5). Tel: 0191 2327734.
Oxford
Ashmolean Museum of Art and Archaeology. Tues–Sat 10–4 (2–4). Tel: 01865 278000
Sheffield
Graves Art Gallery, Surrey Street 1. Tues–Sat 10–5. Closed Sunday and Monday.
Tel: 0114 2735158
Mappin Art Gallery, Weston Park. Wed–Sat 10–5; (11–5); Closed Mondays and Tuesdays.
Tel: 0114 2768588
Ruskin Gallery, 101 Norfolk Street. Tues–Sat 10–5. Closed Sunday and Monday.
Tel: 0114 3735299
Southampton
Art Gallery, Civic Centre. Tue–Fri 10–5; Thu 10–8; Sat 10–4 (2–5). Closed Mondays.
Tel: 01703 223855 769
Swansea
Swansea Museum Service, Glynn Vivian Art Gallery and Museum, Alexandra Road. Tues–Sun 10–5. Tel: 01792 655006

LONDON GALLERIES

British Museum
Great Russell Street WC1B 3DG. 10–5 (2.30–6). Tel: 0171 6361555
Courtauld Institute Galleries
Somerset House, Strand, London, WC2R 0RN. 10–6 (2–6). Tel: 0171 8732526
Dulwich Picture Gallery
College Road SE21. Tue–Fri 10–5; Sat 11–5 (2–5). Tel: 0181 6935254
Iveagh Bequest, Kenwood
Hampstead Lane NW3. Apr–Sep 10–6 (10–6); Oct–March 10–4 (10–4). Tel: 0181 3481286
Leighton House
12 Holland Park Road W14. Mon–Sat 11–5.30. Closed Sunday and public holidays.
Tel: 0171 6023316
William Morris Gallery
Lloyd Park, Forest Road E17 4PP. Tue–Sat 10–1. (1st Sun of the month 2–5). Tel: 0181 5275544
ext. 4390
National Gallery
Trafalgar Square WC2N 5DN. 10–6, Wed 10–8 (12–6). Tel: 0171 8393321 (Publications 0171
8391912)
National Portrait Gallery
St Martin's Place WC2H 0HE. 10–6; (12–6). Tel: 0171 3060055
The Queen's Gallery
Buckingham Palace SW1. 9.30–4.00. Tel: 0171 9304832
Tate Gallery
Millbank SW1P 4RG. 10–5.50 (2–5.50). Tel: 0171 8878000 (Publications 0171 8345651/2)
Victoria and Albert Museum
Cromwell Road SW7. Tues–Sun 10–5.50. Mon 12–5.50. Some Wednesdays, selected galleries
open until 9.30 pm.
Wallace Collection
Manchester Square W1. 10–5 (2–5). Tel: 0171 9350687